Selected Poems

To
Tomos, Gwyn, David and Lewis

Ruth Bidgood
Selected Poems

SEREN BOOKS

SEREN BOOKS is the book imprint of
Poetry Wales Press Ltd.
Andmar House, Tondu Road
Bridgend, Mid-Glamorgan

*Cataloguing in Publication Data
for this title is available from the British Library*

ISBN: 1-85411-069-1

*The publisher acknowledges the financial assistance of the
Welsh Arts Council*

Typeset in 11 Point Palatino by The National Library, Aberystwyth

Printed by:
The Cromwell Press, Wiltshire

COVER PHOTOGRAPH: 'Path in the Valley' by Margaret Salisbury

Contents

New Poems - Valley-before-Night

B+T 10/94

from: 'The Given Time' (1972)

from: 'Not Without Homage' (1975)

from: 'The Print of Miracle' (1978)

from: 'Lighting Candles' (1982)

from: 'Kindred' (1986)

Breaking Bowls

The Maya broke bowls,
smashed weapons, shredded clothes,
killed them, to let their souls go free
into the owner's eternity.

It seems less naïve a concept
than stocking a tomb with toys,
mirrors, cooking-pots, or a ship
with gold armour.
                  We crunch and stumble
through a dark archway, over shards,
splinters, rags of a life, taking
(as we were warned) nothing with us,
except an idea of completeness, an intuition
of light, perhaps a welcome
for the little souls of things
flying free to meet us.

Child at a Gate

On coal-gritty Back Lane
was a black iron gate, tall as our wall.
I remember that height, narrowness.
Bars reaching above me were dull
against blue incandescence
of hovering summer.

I was trying to get in.
The latch fought passively
with my stubby hands.
Something was sliding, scratching
on the grit. Something was coming
breathily nearer. I looked sideways.

It took no notice of me
as it came on —a big black dog
with a white bundle in its mouth,
paper twisted, softened with mouthing,
stained with mud, green slime, blood.
Nearer — no, not paper — a feathery thing
dripping salver and blood — a white duck
smashed, mauled: the dog's yellow teeth
sunk into softness: blood oozing,
dripping on black grit: eyes glazing
but not dead: the dog's eyes
alive, staring ahead: scratchy sound
receding now, of sliding grit:
blood-smears soon hardly to be seen
drying on the coaly lane.

The dull bars laid their pattern on blue.
The latch at last capitulated,
grudgingly letting me through
into the changed garden.

Words

'Go back!' she said, 'Go back!'
and the shape obeyed, fading
backwards through the oak door.
Telling me, she confessed
to lack of courage, love,
even curiosity. She wished she had spoken
words that reached out, gave hope, solved something.
I know that wish and that regret.

Tonight the telephone brings
a man's controlled voice, out of his dark.
Just heard, a tremor wordlessly
asks me for words I cannot find.
Something unquiet has passed a barrier
and is with me. Tentative,
inarticulate, I offer
my listening, my inadequate goodwill,
my wordless hope to meet his wordless fear.

'Amon Ra wakes for us when we sleep'

(Egyptian Book of the Dead)

Not a god only; we too
have sleepers to wake for.
I remember that half-bare sapling
in the autumn hedge, on the day
I heard of your death: counting leaves,
brown and yellow, as though it mattered
to number them for you.

                Over the years
I have lost that clarity, yet still some days
I wake for more than myself: rehearse
hill-names, Allt-y-Bryn, Cefn Coch, Clyn:
hear newly the challenge of stone to water
and water's long sure answering: greet
as a wonder a cheerful mongrel
reeking of horses.
                Is there
reciprocity? At times it seems
the sleep we fall towards is nursed
into an eager morning by some who wake.
The small dog barks, sharp notes proclaiming
now, here. Known day shines on leaves
of birch and thorn, on Cefn Coch, the Gwesyn stream,
the numbered stones.

'I'm here to get away from myself'
(Hotel guest)

She takes a climbing track
scented, shut in, by fir and pine.
From a high corner, landslip
has churned a chaotic ride
all the way down to the valley floor,
making a vertical stripe
of wide-world brightness. Afterwards,
higher, again the forest closes in,
its night of naked underwood
lit here and there by streaks of sun.

Insistent comes the scent
of hot needles, opening cones.
Insistent comes her heartbeat, like the pad
of the draggled old bitch-hound, self,
that rejected slinks at her heel,
humbly, relentlessly following
for the small accepting pat
disgust will not let her give.

The Spout

Rain and rain had followed snow.
Under watery sun, sluggish water
spread, slid on the hill-slope:
churned narrow, brown in ditches:
sucked our steps between tussocks.
The river went in new white violence
over the rocks and down.

The children were tired of wet plodding.
Fields were rutted, grey-brown,
a mess of plashiness; one only,
steeply tilted, showed green.
Thankful for easy walking,
we idled across it.

Just before the gate, we saw grasses
gleam and part. A newborn spout
sprang up, sparkled, flowed.
It spoke to the children. They laughed, screamed,
bathed muddy hands, patted the spout,
attacked it, tried to force it back down,
jumped on it, over it, into it.

A skyful of water, a landful of water,
a dayful of water; and the little spout
could do this! The dismal downwardness
of mud, cheating slitheriness
of surface puddles, demented downrush
of rivers, were gathered, embraced, redeemed
by the small eager spout,
the thrusting, humorous creature of water,
that irrepressibly proclaimed
upwardness, happy intransigence,
in the depth of things.

Mind the Horses!

For Tomos

September has given a sunny day
for the Show. Summer clothes
blossom at last, along green lanes
between cars and horse-boxes.

We are squashed in a hot marquee.
'Don't like it here', says the small boy,
tugging. We go out into thinner noise
and warmth of the field. He pulls me
to dark-faced, dark-eared Suffolks,
deeply bleating in their close pen.

The tremor of hoofs alerts us. 'Mind the horses!'
cry parents to children. We run to look,
and round they come on the track ringing the field—
bright-harnessed, the splendid trotting-ponies,
each rider crouched on a speeding sulky.
Slim legs go spanking by, spokes blur,
colours spin into each other. Minds, hands, reins
implore 'Faster!' and faster they go.

Gripping my hand, smiling, 'Another!', he says,
'Another!', amazed at such riches of speed.
On the hills all round us, far away yet
but nearing, in lessening circles
the horses of winter are up and running.
Mind the horses, my dear, oh mind the horses!

Carreg yr Adar (Rock of the Birds)

Jettisoned in molinia by the river
near the Rock of the Birds,
the rags of his body had long begun
their measured rot towards
clean bone, blown dust
when after weeks another walker
came over the moors.

A jet-plane momentarily
tore silence open.
The skeletal dog, still on guard,
did not flinch. At last
it was coaxed away.
Memory stayed inaccessible
in its head's cave—
a howling song in an alien mode,
still faintly echoing.

Soon the body
was gathered up and gone.
New grass would grow, knowing
only air, rain, dew, the excrement
and paw-press of the hill's creatures.

***

The Rock of the Birds juts out
from eastern slope to stream,
half-bars the valley. A stony path
creeps round it by the river.
To the north, feeder-streams debouch
in a waste of stones.
Little crumbled houses
are shapes of an old summer life,
dairies in no rich pasture,

no green idyll.
One is a perfect oval,
an open eye questioning heaven.

***

Last night, summer rain
soaked our bedplace. He laughed,
pulling me to him. But this morning
the smoored fire was out,
peat-ash a mess of unchancy black,
and my butter puddled with rain.

He was at work all day
at his bunching and patching
with the reeds. The cattle
cropped the grudging grass.
I left the hut,
searching for stumps of bogwood,
strength for the re-lit fire.
There was a man
walking away downstream,
dog at heel. Nor man nor dog
seemed like any I knew;
but they were far at the edge of sight,
and soon gone.

Tonight we lie warm, dry,
under the mended thatch.
The butter is pearled
only with its own sweet sweat.
I have woken, hearing faintly
a howling far downstream.
I lie closer to my sleeping man,
warm, but with open eyes
questioning the night.

***

Here are shifting streams,
stones studding old riverbeds:
named streams
dropping, dawdling, dropping
down rocky channels
out of the moors, ancient lands
of stone-heavers, mound-men.
By streams of the Bull, the Crow,
Sow, Curlew, Wolf-bitch, Stag,
priests of the mound-men danced
unsparing strength of bird and animal
into the tribe, that it might live.

***

I wear the feathered cloak
I am beak-faced.
I range the valley
to tear and gorge.
I do not spare the half-born lamb
or the still-breathing ewe.
I do not spare the body of a man.

***

From the small town he turned
south into the hills. The dog
ran ahead, or padded at heel,
sometimes pushing its long nose
against his hand.
                    Their passing
was a hardly perceptible
imperfection in silence.
Once a jet tore the sky. Once

came the rasping cry of a crow,
calling its mate to carrion.

Unhurried, unfaltering, man and dog
followed their appointed way
across the hills, over the little streams,
down-valley to the Rock of the Birds.

Allt yr Hebog

I went back today, after years,
up three fields and along the hill
to the high shelf above steep woods:
grey outcrop I used to make
my waymark: rushy spring: raised
grassy rectangle with a name
but no history, even here.

Unwise, often, such a return;
and there were changes — a barbed fence
impeding the half-lost path:
below house-mounds, the tumbling track
choked now with rotting boughs,
years of muddy leaves.
                    But up there,
over blue valleys blurred
by the low sun's pale winter blaze,
it was the same — shock of stillness,
and something that escaped naming.
'Peace' would leave out echoes and light:
light above all, as if a life
that had been lived there spun the light,
wove, wore it.
                    As I went down,
sun still outlined high oaks
by the drop to river and road.
Before long, between one tree-root step
and the next, evening began.
                    Above,
dusk slowly took outcrop and spring.
Someting escaped into its own dimension
and danced, swirling soft skirts of light
over the blind hill.

Leaving

They carried her from the door
down the path. The stretcher jolted
at the small gate, but she kept quiet.
All the way to the ambulance that waited
at the end of the narrow track,
she stared up at branches
dancing backwards on a windy sky.

She had been alone for years,
the trees her love, her fear,
her endless conversation.
Outside, the world changed
and did not change. In pictures
she saw it bleed. Around the house
the year's autumnal blood
seeped from tree to ground,
and spring's new combatant growth
played politics of survival.

Branches blurred now above her.
The wide sky she had forgotten
came nearer; millions of unseen worlds
swung into patterns of dance.
Into those huge compulsive rhythms
step by jarring step she was borne on.

Earth Tremor

There was a muffled sound, like a train
tunnelling through the hill.
Daffodils in a vase on the table
shuddered for long seconds, long enough
for incredulity to crystallise.

As the small world stabilised
came, illogically, a sense that this
had been something incurred
five minutes, five years ago,
by doing or not doing — a step
not taken, decision bedevilled;
as if it were better to feel guilty
and thankful than know fire-hearted earth
ungovernable, even here.
                    The still daffodils,
never so soft, so crisp, so yellow,
shone, reprieved.

Bookmark

A blurred snapshot cut to bookmark size
shows a small naked boy, a girl
seal-sleek in her prized swimsuit,
scrambling up a stream. Fern and foxglove
shade and dwarf them. Clutching slippery rocks
they lean forward in a never-passing
moment of effort. Ahead, the sunny grass
they reached and long ago forgot
waits for the press of their wet bodies.

The slip of fuzzy colour-print
already droops dog-eared. Keep it
in a dull book on the top shelf,
almost as safe, almost as hidden
as handgrip in rock, footstep in water,
shadow in springing grass.

Bull in the Nine-acre

Yes, he said, this was the home farm,
and that gaunt jaggedness down the field
all that was left of the big house.
'See that wall? I built that from the stones.'
Handy, the old house; always stone
for building, patching.
'And my daughter found fossils
built into the house, like.
We took a lot of stones for them.
She carried fossils to college —
weighed down, she was, with stones.'
I saw a girl bear through the city
old stolen certainties, older
embedded shapes of life,
to academic judgment.

I photographed the broken structures
of obscure potentates.
Huge black silage-bags
bulged into the viewfinder;
I leaned and weaved to dodge them.
'The bull's in the nine-acre —
better go back the way you came.'
I left prudently, not outstaying
my limited welcome. But I thought
that was a bull of the mind, a device
to deliver old stones, old violations
from too complete a recording,
too rigid judgment; and felt no need
to hurry past the gap
to the nine-acre field.

Lotus

Bryn, the round hill,
dips to a valley that accepts
others: a place of joining.
No wind carries up
conversation of rivers.
Old sheepwalks, hardly grazed,
stretch to the verge of forest.
On this grey day
no smoke rises
from the one gaunt house.

Surely the silent utterance
of this place is 'Emptiness',
its time 'Never'?
Yet it is said
that not leaves, not petals,
but the space at the centre
of the heart's lotus
contains everything.
                Here
rivers out of sight
have their felt rhythms,
like blood through the heart.
Stillness throbs with the flow
of unperceived lives.

This is a place of joining,
whose silent utterance
is 'Abundance',
whose time is 'Ever'.

Village Party

Old sheets are hung like tapestries
on the tall room's peeling walls. Clusters
of blue balloons strain at their tether,
bounce gently on currents of draught.
A great Christmas tree rears up
towards roof-beams and naked bulbs.
So much light! Surely walls
cannot hold it; light will seep
through them, out over dark fields
to amaze the still sheep. So much sound!
The children are beyond themselves.
Now comes a green man
with cap and bells and a guitar,
its massive reverberations
felt through floorboards, and flung back
from rocking roof, unstable walls,
to build an unbearable crescendo.
Children laugh, hammer, jingle bells,
crash, stamp, shout, shout, shout.
One or two at the back of the room
are silent. Over the cheerful gallimaufry
they stare at a high window
where, black on dark,
just seen past reflected light,
is a movement of branches
in towering night.

Oil-spill, 1991

The cormorant can heave itself
from the black beach, over the low wall,
and run about the tarmac till it dies.
Or it can let the thick strange sea
slurp at it till it sags and dies.

The camera zooms in
on punk-spikes of oiled feathers
and the no-understanding,
no-reproach, of round unblinking eyes
that say nothing, simply see,
and see now this last thing.

Sources

a. County History

Llangynog

Small, bleak and barren,
with a ruinous church,
wrote the historian, apologising
for noting a place devoid
of history or good soil,
whose few frugal farmers
would gaze down mortified
from their snowy hills
at the soft flocking-in of green
to the spring valley.

Cold and late, in greyness,
over a field of wet red earth
I draggle to barbed wire
and a ditch. Beyond the trees
Cynog's roofless church
suffers a long shedding of stone.
I free an earthbound cross,
prop it against rubble.
Wind seeps through shelter-trees.
Consecrated silence welcomes in
a flock of prayers crying,
praises clapping their wings.

***

b. Probate

To Thomas Price

You were here, Thomas,
two and a half centuries back,
lordling of a stony acreage:
in your plain rectangle of house,
your nurturing barns,
your yard where the wind caught its breath
and bore on down-valley.

Fatherless, only son,
you wielded a brother's potestas
over your sisters' likings.
Barely yourself of age, you were set
to rule their sullen ripening.

I riffle the writings, searching
for a word more of you.
You were here, Thomas;
I will set down such small dry words
as I find of you, proclaim
against the brag of chaos
a tiny clarity.

Now! now! as you knew it
comes that catch in the wind
and the long howl of its dying.

***

c. Chancery

Opening music

Long parchments and limp inky scraps
corded together, the documents wait.
I smooth and sort, remembering
suddenly a long-forgotten shiver
and challenge, new piano-pieces
my teacher used to open for me,
smoothing the stiff pages;
and the music starting in my head
before a note was played.

Somewhere in this dusty bundle
he waits, old Benjamin, crusty and half-drunk
in his Radnorshire kitchen.
                'Did he throw the will
on the fire, and did you pluck it off?'—
'No', says the widow, badgered
by the Commissioners (making her mark
on the hesitant deposition), 'not on the fire
as they aver, yet he did throw it on the floor,
having cut off the seal; and then again
picked it up and pinned it together
and bade me keep it locked in the coffer
till it should be needed'.
'But did he take a disgust,
a disinheriting disgust, to Charles his heir?'
'Not a disgust', she says, 'yet he was somewhat
in a fret, and I would not bring the will
that night, when he was in liquor;
but next day he did as I have said'.

This music has waited for me to smooth its pages
and stumble into halting interpretation
of tentative harmonies, broken phrasing,
less-than perfect cadences. In my head
I hear what my best skill can never show —
the true notes, played with love.

***

d. Recusant Records

Sectarian

I, Gunter of Gwenddwr,
being of the Old Faith, and for that
much hedged and strictured
and my lands bled of just profit,
have still the advowson
of that heretical conventicle
they call their Parish Church—
church once indeed, but now defiled
by false opinion and mock sacrament.
I catch at a name, give them one
Walter Powell. Up goes their shriek
and cavil — Powell utters no Lord's Prayer,
reads them no Gospel. They will have Prydderch,
Thomas Prydderch or none. Fools!
As though Powell or Prydderch
or any other from the rabble
of bastard ministers unblest
by Christ's apostles could serve
to pull them heavenwards! What care I
for their lamentable capers,
their clownish clerks? One of my bull beasts
would be good enough for them.

(Note: The last sentence of the poem was actually spoken by Bodenham
Gunter, or so says the county historian.)

***

e. In the Field

Visit to the mine

'Did anyone die here?' called the boy
from the crest of the old spoil-heap
in a spruce-glade. I told him I'd heard
of no death; and thought
'except of work, except of hopes'.

The rusty top of the old pump
rose from the floor of a grassy pit,
the shaft they filled and left
(on the bare hill then)
one hundred and thirty years ago.
                    They had gone
to ninety feet here, begun an adit,
sunk another shaft out to the west —
we came on it, dark in forestry.
There was green water some way down,
that seemed slimy with frog-spawn.
'How do the frogs get out?'

The boardroom gloomed over reports —
little lead, less copper

(though the cascading streams we had struggled up
had rust-red pools, and there were gleams
of silver-grey in dull rubble
under pressing trees).

　　　　　　Small and speculative,
the mine was easy to forget.
The men hoisted picks and packs,
headed west and south
to Cardiganshire or Rhandirmwyn.

Decade after decade,
the small detritus of failed enterprise
lay out in the hill winds,
until the planting of these
insistently elegiac trees.
'Spooky', said the boy, happy to leave
as we set off downstream, over the fence
and onto open hill.

　　　　　　The brook
gathered itself, swelled, and close beside
our precarious path leapt forty feet
down slippery crags into the lower valley.
By the pool at waterfall's end
was the cave-mouth of an adit,
shallow, soon abandoned. The water
swirled past and on. Alongside it
we picked our way towards an easier path.

Resurrection Angels

(Kilvert was told that the people used to come to the Wild Duck Pool on Easter
morning 'to see the sun dance and play in the water and the angels who were at
the Resurrection playing backwards and forwards before the sun'.)

These were not troubling the waters
to bring healing. They were serving
no purpose. After the watch at the tomb,
the giving of good news, they were at play.
To and fro went the wings, to and fro
over the water, playing before the sun.

Stolid-seeming villagers stared
enchanted, watching sun dance and play,
light-slivers splinter water's dark.
In dazzle they half-saw
great shining shapes swoop frolicking
to and fro, to and fro.
                                This much was shared,
expected; day and place had their
appropriateness, their certainties.
The people had no words to tell
the astonishment, the individual bounty —
for each his own dance in the veins,
brush of wings on the soul.

Cloud

We were driving home. On either hand
a few houses slid backwards into dusk;
a chapel, an inn went by,
then spring hedges, almost leafless,
dimly flanked our road.
Above was a still palely-glowing sky.

Then to the left puffed up a cloud —
blue-black, vast, grotesque,
a swollen, snout-rearing beast —
to dwarf our journeying, all we saw,
all we could think or say.
It grew, changed, filled the whole
marchland of earth ahead,
till like a dark range of barrier hills
it blocked the future. Still
above it faintly glowed the heights of sky.

Vestigial light picked out a name,
Beulah. Only the name was known.
This was not the plain village of everyday,
set against fields, open and sane.
This was a place hunched under dark,
servile, half-stifled by pressure
of those apocalyptic hills of cloud.
Beulah! The sign was a shout of warning.
Warily we drove through, turned right,
burrowed up-valley into unthreatening night.

Emu's Egg

Trudging through rain along the windy hill
to pull a snarled-up lamb, whistle the dogs
to their flat-out looping of the ewes,
he nursed the notion of Australia —
heat, space, a chance of more
than his hard-earned Breconshire pittance.
Idea became plan, was told,
marvelled at, acted on. He was best friend
to my old neighbour's grandfather,
turned to him for help — a horse and cart
to Liverpool. Northwards they rattled,
through Builth, Newtown, Welshpool. At Liverpool
came a fraught moment. 'John', he said,
tears not far, 'John, sell the horse and cart,
come with me!' For a moment
that far-off sun shone for his friend too,
coaxing; then it was dimmed
by green damp, more deeply penetrating.
'No', said John, 'I can't, I can't'; turned south
through Welshpool, Newtown, Builth again.

John was dead by the time
a letter came, and an Australian parcel,
exotic, unique — an emu's egg,
black, the size (his children said)
of two teacups put together.
It stayed at the farm for years,
then got broken. For a while
they saved the fragments of shell; the story
lasted a little longer. Unlikely transmitter,
I set it down, feeling perhaps for both
brave dreamer and chicken-hearted friend —
one who forced a dream to live, and one
who missed for ever his black two-teacup egg.

Llanfihangel

Some still remember the rose-window
shining through dusk, the bells
that played hymn-tunes, the one
that tolled for the valley's dead.
Splendid Victorian folly, the church itself
lived less than a century. Soft stone
sopped up the endless rain. Above cross-point
of nave and transept, heavy tower
made an infinitesimal shift, chancel arch
moved a millimetre out of true.
In the pulpit, an intermittent drip
punctuated sermons. Whisper by whisper
flaking began, softest of plaster-fall
from pillar and wall, drift of dust
on chaliced wine. Then as a doomed mind,
whose tiny eccentricities have given
little unease, suddenly lurches to grosser
irrationality, the building shed
a first sodden chunk of facing-stone,
and was put away.
Damp barricaded silence lasted
till the slow thudding months of demolition,
the final blasting of the tower.
Grass, yew-trees, graves remain,
and in a few old minds regret
no longer sharp, but steady as rain
that brought down stone and fed the flood of grass.

Rhyd y Meirch

(Note: *Hwyl* — roughly 'enthusiasm' — an incantatory preaching style. *Duw cariad yw* — God is love. The 'washers at the ford' in Celtic legend were omens of death in battle. They washed the shirts of those about to die.)

There seems nothing now
but slow swell of hill,
flow of grass,
bleak lake where men dug clay
for a dam's core.
A narrow road strikes south
for Capel Saron.
The farm Rhyd y Meirch is long gone,
remembered as little
as the battle that bloodied grass
nine hundred years ago.

All names in this quiet valley
speak of war —
Rhyd y Meirch, ford of war-horses:
Rhiw Felen, blood-coloured hill;
Maes Galanas, field of slaughter.
A small wind strokes, rain washes.
Are names all that remain?

Is this silence peace, or a held
violence? or perhaps an empty pan,
its brimming hate spilled, outward-flowing?
The little wind strokes, rain washes,
names are soft on the tongue.

***

I was the soft one; useless,
my brothers would say.
They mocked me when I turned sick
at the gush and smell of the blood.

We always killed the pig on the barn steps.
Even if I had an excuse to go
up the hill, I could not escape
the long squealing and its end.
We kept a pan for the blood.
Little was wasted, and that
soon swilled from the steps;
yet to me they seemed stained
year-long. Son of a farm,
bred to no other life,
I had a changeling's disgust
for our creatures' tortured births
and messy deaths.
Castration, marking, horning —
their lives leaked blood. Something
in the place itself had stained my mind.

***

At the ford
generations of women
knelt at the washing,
rubbing clothes on stones,
lifting into wind, plunging again
into chill water of Camddwr
that rinsed out mud and dung
but left on the men's scrubbed shirts
a faint rusty stain of blood.

***

Rain swirled through trees
beyond the clear windows
of Capel Saron.
Sabbath clothes in crowded pews
smelt of damp and horses.
The preacher's voice rose in the *hwyl*.

He saw blood-washing of sins,
he strove with words to bring us all
into that joy.
Again the word pulsed through my head —
'Gwaed...gwaed...' — 'Blood...blood...'.
I was jammed between two of my brothers,
all crushed among bodies of neighbours and kin.
I struggled giddily to rise. Angrily
Emrys pushed a way for me
to the saving door.
            Hunched in drizzle
on wet grass, I saw again the painted words
over the pulpit, *'Duw cariad yw'*;
and muttered like a fool
'Wash me in rain, my God, my God,
wash me in rain'.

      ***

Nobly rode the princes.
Their cause was just vengeance
for the death of a prince.
Eagerly their men
thronged the valley,
a hosting unrivalled,
wild for the right.
Fiercely their enemies met them,
calling like them on God.

Blood on the hill, blood at the ford.
The day passed; silence came.

The valley's windblown rain
washes and washes at the stain.

Catching Up

The grubby room is almost empty.
Her chair is an island on bare floor.
She is not poor. She has chosen in age
to throw away a life's dead weight.
Rugs, rosewood, silver, translucent bowls
have all gone (to the unworthy, some think).
On her narrow bed, a mound shifts,
furtively, under the greyish cover, mews.

I remember her immaculate —
brown hair scraped back, pinned relentlessly:
eyes sharply judging: tenderness
kept for pampered, pampering gewgaws.
Now white rough-cut hair
hangs softly round her gentler face;
eyes are young, see far; grimy hands
unclench and lie content.

On a tiny television screen,
into loving dark of summer woods
children run through meadow grass.
It has taken years to catch up;
she sees them just ahead,
the width of a field away.

Green Man at the Bwlch

For a week or more
some baffling serendipity
has brought him to me
in books, journals, photographs —
a splay-mouthed face,
flesh shared with leaves.

Now on a remote pass above trees
of two Radnor valleys
I come to this ancient place —
cruck house half-crumbled, lovingly encased
by scaffolding and plastic sheets, cocoon
in which goes on the work of rebirth.
He is here too.

In a central room, on the beam
over the great hearth, royally
he spreads his mouth-borne branches,
meets my unsurprised eyes.
Here is an abyss, like Nietzsche's,
into which if I look long
I find it looking into me.

The terror is in his utter
neutrality. Yet somewhere
in his kingdom of possibilities
is a tree whose leaves give shelter,
whose boughs know songs, whose sap
flows gold through our veins.

Lost Cousin

He was the lost cousin,
the one I never met,
the curly blond three-year-old
who died in his sleep.
We had a photograph of him,
white-skirted but boyish,
turning to smile into the lens.
I pieced together the story
from grown-ups' mutters, evasions —
the 'lovely boy' who had 'little fits',
and in one of them fell asleep
irrevocably, becoming
loss, grief, legend.

A lifetime later
I find I got it wrong
all those decades ago.
He died, but not at three,
not curly, beautiful and tiny,
but twelve years old.
It was I who was small
when we met — for we did; here
is the proof, a pale brown phtotgraph
of a schoolboy, ten or so
(two years to go), mischievous,
healthy-looking, with two younger brothers,
and me, a fat bundle in my father's arms.

Irrationally, I feel I owe him —
what? Nine unremembered years?
What would my truer recollection
have availed him, or me?
It seems there is a sort of peace
in knowing what I had not always known;
in matching fact with pictures in the mind,

as if to remember accurately
could be a tribute bright and soft as flowers.

Valley-before-Night

(Note: The upper Camarch Valley in the old parishes of Abergwesyn and Lla-
nafan used to be a community of some sixteen farms. Only Llednant is still a
working farm. Most of the houses are ruined or demolished. Coedtrefan is
still occupied — Robin, Hazel, Tomos and Gwyn are the only children who
now live in the valley. The local name for the Camarch Valley is *Cwm-cyn-Nos*
— the before-night valley, Valley-before-Night. *Cyheuraeth* — howling (a
death-omen, auditory equivalent of the corpse-candle). *Dechreunos* — begin-
ning-of-night (a custom prevalent here till the second world war).

***

'Why Cwm-cyn-Nos?' No-one's answer
seemed complete. 'It was best
to be home in that valley, or out of it,
before night', one said, adding 'perhaps'.
Another, 'There was never a road
up the Camarch, till the Forestry came'.
One man quietly said 'That is a dark valley'.

***

Looking down from the pass
I saw the valley shiver with light.
Even swathes of spruce, obscuring
paths, fields, old stones,
rose quivering into sun. The river danced
with brilliant daytime candles, omens
of nothing but heat. Yet even then
(was it because I knew that name?)
there seemed a darkness of obliquity,
enigma. Outlines blurred,
as in a photograph of fir-tree tops,
that always looks shaken. For a moment
I read the place as a cryptogram
for danger. Soon the fancy was gone. I saw
only innocent light brimming a green bowl,
and time on time in a subaqueous dance.

***

Griffith Thomas of Cefn Gilfach went to Rhaeadr market
 to buy iron pots for his son's marriage-gift.
Returning over the moors in heavy summer rain, at the
ford over the Camarch below his house he was swept
away by a sudden wild up-swelling of the river.

Coming home late one evening from shepherding,
William Arthur of Blaencwm saw a light dance on the river
between Carregronw and Fedw, and hurried on.

Near that spot the next day was found the body of Grif-
fith Thomas.

***

Coedtrefan: Robin

They sounded the death
in daytime night of the trees.
'Can I go?' he had asked.
We stood by the fence,
watching him run down the field.
Alders by the river hid him; then
there again was the red shirt,
small on the farther hill, as his hurtling rush
dwindled to a laboured climb.
A few riders distantly manoeuvered,
scattering over the hillside:
dogs arrowed towards the wood,
disappeared inside.
Soon came that horn-call;
suddenly all was still,
horses and riders enchanted
into a triangle inverted.
Near its apex, a red splash

46

marked where the boy stood,
motionless too, facing the trees.
Only the river ran on.
We could not hear the worrying,
tearing, of the ritual kill.
What he saw, heard, we do not know.
He came back chastened, with little to say.
The younger ones jostled and laughed;
soon he was laughing with them,
the still moment with its burden of death
given to the river flowing always
through night at the back of the mind.

***

Thomas Thomas of Cluniau died far from the Camarch, at
Merthyr Cynog on the Epynt hills, and was carried on a
wagon for burial at Abergwesyn. One night when he lay
still breathing, waiting his time, his corpse-candle was
seen, going home before him.

***

Who saw the corpse-lights dance
for the death of the farms?

***

Four miles up from Dôlaeron bridge
Cedney flows in, on its bank Pencae.
Twenty years back the shepherd Evan
spread starched white fire of tablecloth
to light the room with ceremony for me,
set china from long-ago markets.
Eleven young ones had grown in that house;

47

two were left, old men. The valley
had scampered with children.
Only the river ran and chattered now.
Two years ago, he said,
a girl on a palamino
had ridden upstream: my daughter.
I felt filaments of time
bind me to her memory and his,
all of us into the valley story.
I left when dark was a hint only,
a growing scent of hay and river-damp,
and did not see him again.

***

Coedtrefan: Hazel

'He won't go!' she grumbled,
ineffectually kicking
the fat pony's sides, her blue gaze
muddled with tears. 'Don't drag his mouth',
her mother called. 'Take him off the track,
up through the trees'. Later
they burst from the wood, chased
alongside us, past us, over the grass.
'He's cantering!' she shouted,
joyful eight-year-old centaur,
part at last of the godling,
filled with beauty and power, her fair hair
flopping, all life riding her way.
Night sent its outriders of cloud
to escort her. She stooped
to the pony's neck in an embrace,
cajoled him to the track, rode home.

'When I was a girl at Pencae',
the woman said, 'my mother
would send me down to Fedw to sleep,
for company for the wife there. Sometimes
her man worked away from home;
she didn't like to be there at night
with only her little ones. I would hurry
down the track, to get there by dark.
She would stir the logs to warm us,
and for light. We ate our food
by the fire, and went to bed
with the children, together,
in a long room in the roof.
We could hear owls, and wind
loosening the birch-leaves; they would go
creeping and dancing over the roof.
But we slept; we were all together.
In the morning I would go home.
My mother would look at me, sharp-like,
and ask, *'A oedd popeth yn iawn yn y Fedw?*
— Was is all right at the Fedw?'

***

Morgan Dafydd of Pencae died from a wound, falling
from his horse on to a little dagger which he had with
him for an evil purpose.

At about two o'clock in the morning of that day,
Rhys Rowland had seen a coffin made of light, stand-
ing outside Morgan's house. Meeting with him later,
Rhys warned him, but in vain.

***

Coedtrefan: Tomos

'No!' he shouts, asleep, in the early hours.
'No!' meeting comfort with anger and fear.
Only his father can help, prising him
from a snarl of blankets, carrying
the tense resistant two-year-old downstairs
and out into moonlight. 'Look, Tomos,
there's the moon' — and slowly
he slackens and nestles, even smiles,
finding this valley night kinder
than the dreamed one, where who know what
old savageries had claimed him
as victim, participant. By day
he is extrovert, charmer,
paying with small change of smiles
for the fears he creates.
'Running, running!' we heard him call;
escaped to a road, he ran laughing,
holding the crown of the way,
straight at approaching wheels.
Silence can mean new danger, a rush
down the field where the small shape
makes for the river, uneasy dogs
keeping pace with him, unsure
whether or no they may block his race
to the creaming dark. Only tiredness
tames him. Patching his scratches
we guess at hurts only dark hours reveal,
and which the pharmacopeia of love
must surely hold a salve to heal.

***

Here at Sychnant, where now is only the skinny disproportion of a broken house, lived the slate-quarry bailiff.
Here died six-year-old William Garibaldi Williams, and went over the pass to lie with others of Cwm-cyn-Nos in the chapel-yard of Pantycelyn.

***

Under the flagstone by the door
of Gilwern was a ghost in a box,
marauding spirit of a Scot
killed for his pack and his cash.
After years, there were rumours
of sounds in the hall, on the stairs.
Men said he had swelled in his rage,
burst free. One day he would choose
his victim. There is no charmer now
to catch and box him.
New owner, summerer, can you repair
moaning hall, groaning stair?

***

Dôlcegyrn: walls by the river, an old tale
of a church St Michael rejected,
whisking stones away by night.
The known was a cottage
with a plum-tree. Pencae children,
on their way down-valley,
would thieve and dodge,
escaping sticky, cock-a-hoop,
pockets squashy with plums.
Dusk holds the swish and pad
of small feet sneaking past
in a hurry, on the long path home.

Coedtrefan: Gwyn

The small grey rabbit executes
an improbable twisting skip
and vanishes behind the sofa.
The baby on the floor
is totally given up to laughter.
Seven months old, native of the valley,
he is happy, humorous,
except when a pain, or hunger,
briefly darkens his life.
His round intent eyes fix constantly
upon the world's myriad appearances,
and feed his brain to satiation.
He does not yet know
ordinary from strange;
he is not vulnerable
to the ambiguities of dusk.
He rolls on his back, smiling up
at plants on the sill, staring
at leaf-shapes against the darkening panes.

***

The many stones at Pantycelyn
grow hard to read, as moss and lichen
impose their freer patterns
on flowing script, grey wings and flowers.

Isaac, son of Isaac Thomas of Fedw, died in February 1812,
aged four. His sister Margaret died next Christmas Day,
aged one year. John Arthur of Caregronw died in 1866
aged ninety-two. Edward Lewis of Pencae, shepherd and
poet, called Iorwerth Camarch, died in 1947 aged sixty-
four.

***

Who heard the *cyheuraeth* for the doomed farms?
Who heard the *cyheuraeth* pass along the valley?

***

The last tenant of Llednant
is old. The Forestry watches him
as a buzzard a failing beast.
Each day now, with its ritual
of feeding, herding, fencing,
is a small battle won
in the war he must lose.
More than his life will end;
he knows it. 'Tomorrow'
means only the next day.
He tends on still unplanted fields
creatures who make no plans,
and fills his tired days
with the quiet of their unawareness.

***

Coedtrefan: Dechreunos

A woman trundles her baby home
as winter sun dips; a little boy
trudges, hand on the pushchair.
Soon, two homing from school
are voices in the wood,
shapes on the track,
squabbling, laughter, at the door.
When dark comes, the house
spills light; on it float
shadows, stretching, retracting.

A man returns. Briefly, the door
lets light gush out. Then
a family is enclosed in light,
the house in the valley night.

Out of the dark they came,
Camarch's people, for *dechreunos*.
Work ended with daylight; then
each night one house,
one only up-valley and down,
would fill itself with light
(every candle lit, every lamp)
for neighbours' sheltered hour
of talk in a luxury of light.
Along darkening paths they came.
Each time the door was opened,
against outflowing of light
a shape of darkness moved in,
silhouette vanishing into light.

Coedtrefan keeps *dechreunos*
for people of invisible houses.
Dark finds its entrance, speaks
to dark of each heart.
Light pours like benediction.
Hands salving present hurts
soothe timeless agonies to sleep.
On spilt light, shadows stretch and shrink.
The children sleep. Beyond an unseen field
Camarch whirls its flotsam on
over chafed stones: flows free of time.

The Given Time

That could have been my time —
the years to come, all meaning gone
from the broken shape of the house,
blurred like a thicker shadow
than tree-shadows in the silent forest;
hardly a shape even — a darkness,
irregularity, among the ordered trees —
not a memory left, not a line of its story.

But in this time decreed as mine,
with hardly a stone yet fallen, the house is lapped
by the first waves of forest-land,
whose crests bear the tiny trees.
The house has lost its life, not yet identity —
it is known hereabouts, stories are still told
of men who lived there. Silent, it poses questions,
troubles me with half-answers, glimpses, echoes.

To accept as mine this given time,
to live the haunted present and know the forest's shadow
is the one way to break from snatching branches,
and back over nursery furrows stumble at last
to where in the winds of the past the house rose whole,
a shape of life in a living valley —
winter brightening the low rooms
with snow-light and spark-spattering logs,
or spring's shadows playing like lambs,
racing with the sun like children over the fields.

Chimneys

Far away, we saw three chimneys in the trees
across the valley, on a little hill
beyond the first hill's shoulder.

Shading our eyes from the sidelong evening sun,
we gazed and guessed till we could almost see
the roofs of beast-house, stable and barn.

No smoke rose from the chimneys, we said at first,
but soon we swore there was smoke, so alive the house
seemed in the dying sunlight.

And afterwards, alone, I searched on maps
to make the house more mine by knowing its name —
and found there is no farm on the hill,

no house of any kind, not even a ruin.
What trick of sun and shade put chimneys there
for us to find and talk about?

And is the evening more real than the house?
Now both are gone, it seems a fine distinction
that one was and the other was not.

Remembering, I build the evening again,
the plunging valley and the little hill,
and look! there are chimneys in the trees.

Little of Distinction

Little of distinction, guide-books had said—
a marshy common and a windy hill:
a renovated church, a few old graves
with curly stones and cherubs with blind eyes:
yews with split trunks straining at rusty bands;
and past the church, a house or two, a farm,
not picturesque, not even very old.
And yet, the day I went there, life that breaks
so many promises, gave me a present
it had not promised — I found this place
had beauty after all. How could I have seen
how a verandah's fantastic curlicues
would throw a patterned shadow on the grass?
or thought how delicate ash-leaves would stir
against a sky of that young blue? or known
trees and grey walls would have such truthful beauty,
like an exact statement? And least of all
could I have foreseen the miles on hazy miles
of Radnorshire and Breconshire below,
uncertain in the heat — the mystery
that complements precision. So much sweeter
was this day than the expectation of it.

Roads

No need to wonder what heron-haunted lake
lay in the other valley,
or regret the songs in the forest
I chose not to traverse.
No need to ask where other roads might have led,
since they led elsewhere;
for nowhere but this here and now
is my true destination.
The river is gentle in the soft evening,
and all the steps of my life have brought me home.

Turner's Painting of Hafod

The delicate fantastic house
gleaming in sidelong light
seems more alive yet less substantial
than the foreground's romantic tangle
of rocks, trees and cascades,
or the looming mass of trees behind.
Straight lines and balanced arches
define the fragile body
of one man's threatened dream
amid the swirling grandeur of chaos.
The painter, prescient, saw the house
as if, its doom acccomplished,
already it haunted the valley and men's minds —
Hafod, luminous as its own legend.

Old Pump-house, Llanwrtyd Wells

The door is open. I shall not be intruding,
going in to sit on the bench by the wall,
to breathe the stuffy dankness streaked with sulphur,
and stare through broken panes over the shaggy grounds.
This sociable place has died through lack of visiting.
A pungent drip, still slowly forced from the spring's heart,
has grown a fungus-garden in the great mirrored basin.
Some chairs lie on the sheep-fouled floor,
some lurch, still conversationally grouped,
against the counter over which was handed
health by the tumblerful when crowds came here,
laughing and garrulous, to take the waters;
pulling faces over the taste of their cure,
and bragging of the glasses they had drunk
like boys about their beer. They came streaming
six times a day from the bursting village
to jostle and gossip round the sulphur-bar.
Sheep-farmers, knitting wives, holiday miners
from the black valleys, jam-packed the houses,
ate meals in shifts, and sat outside singing hymns
on the suddenly hushed street of evening;
or went back in warm dusk to the well-house
to hear the Builth harper play under summer trees
and watch the youngsters dance.
The plucked notes, never wholly gay, and laughing voices
spiralled up through the trees, up the long valley;
and lost themselves among the hills
over the sealed frontier of the past.

Manor House

Do not reject this fading house
and say its beauty suits a decadent taste.
Much is dying here, but to miss the swan-song
keeps nothing alive, blasphemes against the moment.

Do not reject this dying house.
It is as lovely over the field of thistles
and crowded round by the too-heavy trees
as one a traveller came to years ago
and found the lawns lit with Lent lilies,
the sundial unbroken telling an old time
at the heart of the weedless garden,
and the boys gone squirrel-hunting in the woods.

Nant y Cerdin

In high morning I am haunted
        by long-ago mornings—
and even those were ghost-ridden
        by a more distant morning,
never quite remembered
        but never dying at noon.
Today when wheatears
        flash from sunny rocks
and new loose-limbed lambs
stagger appalled through the stony stream
        after stolid ewes;
when daffodils blow in the nettle-garden
        of a farm with broken windows,
and in a remote brown valley
the clammy standing stone
        grows warm to touch —
even today ghosts come
        whispering of a ghost.
Could there ever be a morning unhaunted,
a spring shining
        with no sunlight but its own?
Only the first, perhaps,
        the lost ideal morning,
the one that must be found,
must be lived or haunt me always,
the lost morning on forgotten hills.

Log Fire

'Come to the fire', say my friends,
moving books and knitting from the settle.
Then I know I am back
after all the hours and miles,
and we sit in a sun-cave,
all heat and brightness.

Light springs from logs, spreads from lamps,
beats back from a wall of brasses —
a charm of light against death-wish darkness
of the upper valley. From the window here,
through tossing boughs we lose and find
one light from the one house braced against wind
laden with snow from the black mountain
that rears twin cairns above a cataract few visit,
in a cold kingdom of black bog and rock.

Men, borderers of such a wilderness,
move on old ritual paths
through predictable seasons.
Faith piled these logs
against the sure coming of snow,
and is now vindicated as the first flakes fall
powerless to chill this warm creation, this evening
on the edge of desolation.

Spiders

She played the piano sometimes in summer,
when westering sunlight through the open window
gave tarnished candlesticks and dusty curtains
a gentle elegance, so that not to age,
not to fade, would have seemed a lapse of taste.
The hesitant arpeggios, broken trills,
brought great shy listeners from the creepered trellis.
Scuttle, and pause, scuttle and pause, came spiders
on tentative delicate legs, to hear the music;
and I, a child, stayed with them, unafraid —
till turning from the yellow keys, one day
she told me of a room where long ago
it had been she who saw the spiders drawn
helpless by threads of music, and listened with them.
Then I felt shut with her into that dream
of endless corridors, rooms within rooms,
mirrors on mirrors compulsively reflected;
while down the corridors, nearer and nearer,
came the great spiders delicately walking.

Stone

Arcadia was never here.
Ice-needles tortured the thin soil,
spring snow lay long by the north wall,
yet the peat-fire had a summer heart.
Waves of life receding left
jetsam of stone — grey megaliths
half-sunk in tussocky grass now
but still processional on the ridge above,
leading into a mystery:
in a cranny of the valley, a ring of stones
that sheltered a hearth once: a roofless hut
of later years, perched high upstream
under the shadow of cairned hills.
The rushes cut each autumn
to mend the thatch, one year
were cut no more; over the centuries
the path was lost. Only stone lasts here.
Stone proclaims life, affirms a future
by virtue of so many pasts,
yet baffles questioning. As I touch walls
warm in the sun today, and feel
so many summers gentle to my hand
and yet withheld, I would crush stone
in my fist, if I could, till truth's milk ran.

Burial Path

When we carried you, Siân, that winter day,
over four rivers and four mountians
to the burial place of your people,
it was not the dark rocks of Cwm-y-Benglog
dragged down my spirit,
it was not the steepness of Rhiw'r Ych
that cracked my heart.

Four by four, Siân, we carried you,
over the mountain wilderness of Dewi,
fording Pysgotwr and Doithïe,
crossing Camddwr by Soar-y-Mynydd,
Tywi at Nant-y-Neuadd; every river passed
brought us the challenge of another hill beyond.

Again and again from his rough pony's back our leader
signalled with his hazel-staff of office
four, breathless, to lay down your coffin,
four, fresh in strength, to bear you
up the old sledge-ways, the sinew-straining tracks,
the steeps of Rhiw Gelynen and Rhiw'r Ych.

I with the rest, Siân, carried you.
The burial path is long — forty times and more
I put my shoulder to the coffin
before the weary journey was accomplished
and down at last through leafless oaks
singing we carried you to the crumbling church,
the ancient yews, at the burial place of your people.

It was not then my heart cracked, Siân,
nor my soul went into darkness.
Carrying you, there was great weariness,
and pride in an old ritual well performed—

our friend's firm leadership, smooth changes
from four to four, the coffin riding
effortlessly the surge of effort.
And at the grave, pride too in showing
churchmen how we of Soar knew well
ways of devotion, fit solemnity.

But with your grave whitened — the last ceremony —
and my neighbours, as I had urged them, gone ahead,
then it was I felt the weight of death
for the first time, Siân, and I knew
it would be always with me now
on the bitter journey that was not yet accomplished.

Now as I went down Rhiw'r Ych alone
and turned west over the ford of Nant-y-Neuadd,
I knew there was only darkness waiting
for me, beyond the crags of Cwm-y-Benglog.
It was then my heart cracked, Siân, my spirit
went into that darkness and was lost.

At Strata Florida

This afternoon on the edge of autumn
our laughter feathers the quiet air
over tombs of princes. We idle
in an old nave, lightly approach
old altars. Our eyes, our hands
know fragments only; from these
the Abbey climbs and arches into the past.
We look up and find
only our own late August sky.

Ystrad Fflûr, your shadows fall
benevolently still on your ancient lands
and on us too, who touch your stones
not without homage. Take our laughter
on your consenting altars,
and to the centuries borne up
by your broken pillars, add
the light weight of an hour
at the end of summer.

Elegy for Sarah

Bitter apples load the tree
by a girl's grave
in a tangle of summer weeds.
Small wet apples glow
through summer rain.

'My days are past'
she cries from her stone,
'my purposes are broken off' —
apple bough broken,
fallen in dripping weeds.

'Even the thoughts of my heart' —
my thoughts, my purposes, my days
broken among weeds,
and summer rain falling
on wet stone, bitter apples.

Stateless

In some nissen-hut of my mind
I have a stacked bed-roll, wooden chair,
suitcase plastered with peeling labels,
and a cheap clock measuring lethargic days.
I have no papers. Sometimes I am offered
forged ones, at too high a price.
Now you come, promising real
identity cards. Forgive me if till they arrive
I think it too early to rejoice.

Letter

Dear Sister, it seems to me long
since I waited last on you
in Summer at your house in Hereford
when we had Converse on manifold subjects
as of our Children and of matters
touching us both. It is much in my mind
today how I did then speak
of my dear Husband, saying
it was great Happiness to see
how having returned out of Hereford
to dwell in these Welsh Mountains
(the which are his Native Land),
he was no longer Sick nor Burthened
in Spirit, but in New Health
and often merry, so that I too
could not forbear to laugh. Although
in very truth this Land of his
was never to my Mind nor Liking,
being far from towns
and much Afflicted with Great Rains and Floods,
and our Mansion House but a Poor Dwelling
with little comfort, by reason of its Age
and the Great Winds in these Hills.
But now my dear Sister it is long
since we spoke thus together
and had much Delight in Converse
on these things, and in the Mild Airs
of that summer. For now all Tranquillity
has left me, since my dearest Husband
is Ill indeed, and of a strange Distemper,
so that we know not what Physic
may profit him, and can but pray
Almighty God to bring him safely through
this Fit of Sickness. And indeed, Dear Sister,

the Great Harshness of the Winter
amid these Rough Welsh Hills
and the long Hours of Darkness
(so that I am sometimes in Terror
that Light should not return, yet chide myself
greatly for such Folly, fit only for Children),
these things weigh heavy upon me
and would so more, but that I must
be always of good Heart in going
unto my Husband, that he may have no Fears.
So my dear sister assure yourself always of my Love
and Thankfulness toward you, and pray to God
for us all, and that we may again
come to your House in time of Summer
as we did heretofore. Your humble Servant
and truly loving Sister, Jane Vaughan.

Sheep in the Hedge

This is no mild and never-never sheep,
but a heavy wild thing, mad with fright,
catapulting at you from a noose of brambles,
hurtling back into worse frenzy of tangles.
Don't imagine you are welcome.
Don't expect gratitude.
That woolly maniac would hate you
if she had any consciousness to spare
from panic. She can see sideways.
There is too much world forcing itself
through slit eyes into her dim brain —
a spiky overpowering pattern of thorns.
Now, worst of all, she suffers the sight of you
(no doubt malevolent), hideously near,
touching her! She wrenches, rips, breaks out,
knocks you into the hedge and is away,
her plump bedraggled body jogging down the road
full-pelt on sticks of legs, pert hooves. You are left
to mop your dripping scratches and stitch up
the tatters of your good intentions.

Hanging Days

Plenty were sorry to see them go,
the shows by Tarell bridge.
Brecon would be full as a skin
on a hanging day —
good for trade, good for the soul.

Thousands would come and wait on the river bank
and on the bridge, staring up
at the gallows under the prison wall.
There was always a sigh when they led him out
to stand under the noose. Every time
something fresh to enjoy, to teach your children —
we have lost a lot, with the old pleasures gone.

There was so much in a hanging, after all —
a warning, and a drama; you could hate
that fellow there — cheat, robber,
murderer, even, on a lucky day —
and pity him too, love him almost.
Choking death would take him today
and stay away from you, perhaps, for that much longer.

And they, of course, the doomed ones,
were in their glory. How they rose
to the occasion! — made improving speeches
to the crowd, forgave the hangman
and everyone for miles! One sang
heart-rending hymns and got us all to join
in harmony: another led in prayer
for half an hour or more — the chaplain
(a new lad, pale already) was quite outfaced.
And the hard ones, decked for death
in delicate finery, or scorning him with their rags —
they gave some splendid moments,
forgiving nobody, refusing clergy,

laughing in the gentry's faces — you could smell
  brimstone!

Myself, it was the girls I would go miles for.
One her prying neighbour found
forcing her baby's corpse into a peat-pool.
Seventeen she was, all eyes in a thin white face.
We had the biggest crowd for months
to see her die. She showed no shame
and would not pray — just gave us back our stares
till she was hooded, noosed, and jerked
into blackness. Who would have missed
such a sinner, such a memory!

Yes, we have lost a lot these days.
It was good to see a death we thought deserved —
our eyes used up that death; for a little while
we felt safe. We were proved wrong
time and again, but still came back
to win our space of peace out of that
permitted violence, now hidden
dirtily in a furtive cell. Death is the same
as ever. It is we who have lost the knack
of looking at him, now that when we meet
we are never sure he is deserved.

Grievance

(A found poem from a manuscript at Shrewsbury Record Office.
The maidservant Alice Owen writes to her parents, 20th May, 1712.)

Dear mother, I wonder at you,
and take it very unkind
that you are so urgent at me
to lay out money for Sidney.
I will not lay out any more money
for them nor nobody else.
Dear mother, consider, I am but a servant
and have nothing but what I work hard for:
therefore I desire you would stop your hand
and solicit no more for nobody,
but consider how young you sent me out
above all the rest, and what hardship I had
to come up on my feet, and yet
I have been a mother and a slave to them all
instead of a sister, and have laid out money —
a crown? Nay, I may say pounds
and not less, and now I think it is time
to shut up and look at home
except I get more thanks for my pains.
I am sure I have had a great care
and taken great pains
to get what I have, and go to my bed
with many an aching heart and bone
and tired limb that you know nothing of,
but you all think that I get money
very easily, and let me undergo
what hardship I will. Methinks you might
have employed your pen in something else
than soliciting for Sidney:
in congratulating me or joining me in prayers
for my safe delivery out of a great rogue's hand

who designed to have ruined and made a beggar of me —
for when he found another man
came into my company, so that he could not
have his desire, then he raised
all the scandalous reports he could
to take away my good name.
That is all one, I see very plain,
out of sight and out of mind,
only so far as serves everybody's turn,
no matter what becomes of me,
sink or swim.

Witness

Talking to his grown-up visiting daughter
opposite me in the train,
he uses me as audience,
half-turns to include me.
She courteously tolerates his questions,
enriches niggardly answers
with a smile. To believe in a bond
with this cool stranger he must have my
complicity. He chatters, covering
uncertainty, invokes minutiae
of a shared past. I am to witness
that they are as close as ever — she
knows they are not. He laughs often,
but his eyes call
'My daughter, my daughter',
after a ghost that dwindles
down-wind.

Messenger

Is there a formula for telling bees
of a stranger's death? They are remote
in the wild upper garden, yet however aloof
and preoccupied, they require to know
of crisis and celebration. They take offence
at a breach of their code, may suffer
a psychosomatic sickness,
swarm inaccessibly, or leave en masse.

The bees do not know me. Today
there is no-one skilled in their wishes
who has time for them; death came unforeseen
to an old man resting here, and broke the calm
of the ordered house. I have no
ritual phrases for this occasion,
but am the only messenger
available. How should I speak to them?

Perhaps they will not expect ceremony
from one who is no concern of theirs.
Perhaps it is permissible to approach,
making as little stir as possible,
through the huge hemlock and old black-currant
    bushes,
and stooping at each white-slatted house
say only. 'Bees, an old man has died —
I do not know his name'.

Tourists

Warner, setting out eagerly from Bath
at five on a lively morning
for the inspiring rigours of Wales
with obliging C........., equipped himself for adventure
with a rusty but respectable spencer
(good enough for North Wales, he said).
The travellers' huge pockets bulged with clothes,
maps, and little comforts; their heads were full
of Ossian, whose horrendous glooms
they were gratified to recognise
one evening on the road to Rhayader
(though Ossian had not prepared them
for the state of the road, or the shortage
of bedchambers at the 'Lion').
Romantic tourists, no doubt, perpetual
outsiders, but willing to love,
and finding much 'singular, striking
and indescribable'. They were comic
(embarrassed at being spotted,
with their pedlars' pockets, by fashionable females),
but worked hard for their exaltations,
plodding twenty-five miles to Machynlleth
north over boggy mountains, or stumbling
two hours across rocks to find a guide
to Dôlbadarn ruins. They were uncomplaining
on Snowdon in a thick mist (they drank milk
gratefully, but longed for brandy), and did not grumble
when, at Aberglaslyn, salmon failed to leap
(only two would even try). Who can say
that at the end of August, leaving Chepstow
for flood-tide at the ferry, they were taking
nothing real away, or that their naïve and scholarly
   wonder
had given nothing in return?

Microcosm

Clearing weeds uncovers under trees
old steps to a choked stream, still bridged
by a stone dragged years ago.
At the garden's end, trees so huge
as to be still in every weather but storm,
and then hardly perturbed, are presences
that contain and exclude.

The house, cherished, takes the sun.
Flower-beds and tended paths make patterns
of purpose quietly achieved, thoughts
controlled, with not too rampant
an undergrowth. But the verge
of lawns blurs into a domain
of abandoned grand designs, small failures,
where nothing is under control. Bindweed
strangles the raspberries, nettles are sly
and savage in the hedge. Lopped rhododendrons
lie, leaves browning, on the fern.
Buttercups jungle-strong have forced their way
between the slats of a garden seat
by a pool imagined but not made.

There is an older beauty here, nearer
the potential of chaos, than in parterre
and ordered path. Schemes failed,
but were made with love; the power
then tapped still flows in the wind
through this profusion of leaf.
Borne up by forces of old hope,
forgotten ideas, unwasted love, the house
rests at a world's heart.

Hoofprints

The legend was always here,
at first invisible, poised above the hill,
stiller than any kestrel. Idle hands
carved hoofprints on a rock
by the hill path. The legend, venturing nearer,
breathed warm as blessing. At last
men recognised it. A magic horse
had leapt from hill to hill, they said,
the day the valley began. Could they not see
his prints, that had waited in the rock
till guided hands revealed them?
From the unseeable, legends leap.
In the rock of our days
is hidden the print of miracle.

All Souls'

Shutting my gate, I walk away
from the small glow of my banked fire
into a black All Souls'. Presently
the sky slides back across the void
like a grey film. Then the hedges
are present, and the trees, which my mind
already knows, are no longer
strangers to my eyes.
The road curves. Further along,
a conversation of lights begins
from a few houses, invisible except as light,
calling to farms that higher in darkness
answer still, though each now speaks
for others that lie dumb.
Light at Tymawr above me, muted by trees,
is all the voice Brongwesyn has,
that once called clearly enough
into the upper valley's night.
From the hill Clyn ahead
Glangwesyn's lively shout of light
celebrates old Nant Henfron, will not let
Cenfaes and Blaennant be voiceless.
I am a latecomer, but offer
speech to the nameless, those
who are hardly a memory, those
whose words were always faint
against the deafening darkness
of remotest hills.
For them tonight when I go home
I will draw back my curtains, for them
my house shall sing with light.

Clehonger Thorn

Woman, I tell you it was blood that ran,
not sap — my axe drew blood!
I'll not touch that thing again,
that devil's thorn, or God's —
let it grow, let it spawn
its pale wrong-season flowers
and draw the gang of gapers here
on each Old Christmas Eve!

Let all the miracle-chasing louts
in Herefordshire come here
trampling my land with lumpish boots
in January night — some huffing in
just before twelve, their breath in their hands!

Blood is nothing when it spouts
from a slaughtered beast, or even
from a man's wound — the one you let flow,
the other you staunch. But what do you do
when a tree bleeds, but pray?

At Nevern

Nevern, signed with David's cross and Brynach's,
lay hushed and innocent. We stood
in the sunny churchyard. Tower and trees
rippled with heat-haze, as if a tiny breeze
passed over baptismal water
in a golden font. On Carn Ingli above,
Brynach walked with angels; the afternoon
was a pause in their conversation.
Silence surrounded the laughter of children
who broke from yew-trees' shadow
to run between the tombs.
Perception reached out to the hills
tentatively as a hand
to a loved face. Unborn words
were given into winged keeping.
In dusk on the northward road
we were too far away to hear
when at the carn the voices began again.

Acquaintance

It was from a border county of my life
you crossed into another country,
having never settled. Smoke rose one dawn
from the overnight house for which
your thrown stone transitorily defined
a patch of my waste land; but soon
the hut was derelict. Acquaintance ending
seems not to warrant uneasier weather
than a fraction of wind-change brings;
yet over my moors the sky sags now,
black with irrational certainty
of departures. From your hasty thatch
rushes loosen, blow east. The heartland may be next
to know depopulation.

Iconoclast

'Take down the Sun and Moon', he ordered,
shutting behind him the day's last church door.
His mare, tethered, turned on him
her simple gaze devoid of censure,
which he was free to think a welcome.
That night he wrote, soberly exultant,
'Today we broke down sixty superstitious pictures,
some Popes and Crucifixes, and God the Father
sitting in a Chair, and holding a Glass in his Hand'.

Listing them on the smug page, he frowned to find
images unbroken in his mind's tabernacle —
'three of God the Father,
and three of Christ and the Holy Lamb,
and three of the Holy Ghost
like a Dove with Wings;
and the Twelve Apostles carved
in Wood on the Top of the Roof,
and Two Mighty Great Angels with Wings'.

Sleep dragged him down to suffer
the trumpeted charge of carven cherubim.
Battered by a thousand wooden wings, he lay
broken, listening in terror, understanding nothing,
while the great Angels he had left for dead
still cried aloud God's message
in the forbidden language of beauty.

Drinking Stone

You offer me your stories
laughing, to show I may laugh, to say
you are sure I must mock
at such old childishness.
Tonight by your fire I listen
to tales of the drinking stone
that each midsummer cockcrow
goes thirsty down to the stream.
I am not to think you credit
that shuddering heave of stone
from the suck of earth, that gliding
over still-dark fields, that long drinking.
You tell it laughing, wary of my response,
but I shall not think you credulous.
It is I who thirstily drink
wonders, I who from dawn mist mould
a grey shape, sated, going home.

Gwlad yr Hâf (Somerset)

'Oh, I could almost reach across!' she would say.
It was so close, my mother's country,
but I would not own it. To see it clearly
meant rain. I stared resentfully
over narrow but unmistakable sea
at those other hills, and refused
to acknowledge kinship. She would coax me
to the window, trying to show me
fields over Minehead way — it was true,
one could see green on those too-clear slopes
in the doomed sunlight. It pained her that I
so rarely wanted to look. I could not speak
of my own nature's alienated lands,
my need to have one coast only, my fear
of the dark weather already drumming
through the straits of my blood.

Standing Stone

The stone stands among new firs,
still overtopping them. Soon
they will hide it. Their lower branches
will find its cold bulk
blocking their growth. After years,
lopped trunks will lie piled,
awaiting haulage. The stone will stand
in a cleared valley, and offer again
the ancient orientation.

The stone stores, transmits.
Against its almost-smoothness
I press my palms. I cannot ask,
having no word of power,
no question formed. Have I
anything to give? My hands offer
a dumb love, a hope towards
the day of the freed valley.
Flesh fits itself to the slow curve
of dominating stone, as prayer
takes the shape of a god's will.

A mindless ritual is not empty.
When the dark minds fails, faith lives
in the supplication of hands
on prayer-wheel, rosary, stone.
It is evening. I walk down-valley
on an old track. Behind me
the ephemeral trees darken.
Among them, the stone waits.

Guest

She strains the fragile evening,
stretching it too far.
Tomorrow's butts and dregs
will be comment enough;
forbearance becomes you.
Her coat, drooping from a chair,
fails to catch her eye;
she is deaf to the broken-backed crash
of the last grey log.
But now, as the garden shivers
in a night-wind from the hills,
she cannot escape grim chatter of leaves
on dark panes, or longer pretend
that the evening is still alive.
Your gentleness, patient with slow goodbyes,
protects her from discomfiture. At last
under her car's rakish pressure
the cattle-grid shakily shouts;
from the encompassment of your windows' lights
she is gone. She sees them once,
through rain, at the turn of the road.
All the way home, they shelter her still.

Film, Aran Islands

In this film of an island from the air
walls make a pattern like leafless ivy-stems,
the island the stone they grip —
stems without hope of growth,
tightly in death resisting
prisings of time and weather.

Man's life rooted, spread, gripped
on this hard island till sap dried.
The walls he left go on
uselessly resisting the salty wind.

The camera tricks us into truth
with its image of a tenacity
reason finds barren, and the heart
coaxes into a yield of small dark berries.

Colour-Slide

I have been sorting slides all day.
What do I remember, this winter evening?
Ten-year-old snow froths up
through a June lake; castles drown in corn.
Child's face and man's, imperfectly echoing
each other, alike chiefly
in vulnerability, surface in turn.
Streets run down to a beach,
all beaches, where selves by the score
laze in a composite summer.
A church, a sorrel-patch, dead friends,
blue ice and a lorry-load of rhubarb
are tossed up and sink back
into the cauldron. One picture
I salvage intact — a lit shed
full of white turkeys fattening,
with three months to live. They are caught
in the everlasting limbo of my slide,
row towering behind row, pink necks craned
and dot-eyed heads all turned
to the encapsulating click. Why have I isolated
this picture from the brew? Perhaps
it is because these creatures' days
were more obviously numbered, and because for them
merciful callousness spares me
too sharp concern. While all I might weep for
in the boxed past is now obscured
in a bubbling of images, these funny birds are clear,
staring, silently gobbling 'Gone, gone, gone!'

May

Here-and-gone shadows in the river
are small trout. Sharp flint,
cutting dark across ripples,
is shadow of a bird.
Hawthorn, tilted
by last winter's gales,
leans like willow,
yields as a sacrifice
the image of its flowers
for blurring by water,
shaking by trout-shadows,
wounding by dark flint.

The language of vulnerable sun
has one word only
for love, give, ask, be,
and in a million evanescent shapes
utters it like a prayer.

Burial Cist

Drought had shrivelled the bogs
on the high moor. Peat dried
uncut, unstacked. A hardness
struck through yellow grass.
Searching for an ancient grave
we scattered, quartering arid acres, peering
into powdery base of tussocks, seeking signs.
Thunder lurked in the huge sky.

From long dykes braced with leaning stones
we sighted the distant fire-hill
across a hidden valley, and called,
launching our small shouts through hot haze,
each hailing another's dark archetypal shape
on the moving skyline. One waved, pointed, ran.
We converged on a broken mound, hardly higher now
that the rough clumps around it.

By the little slab-lined grave,
open and empty, we were silent.
Below the moor the crags, below the crags the road
and the coming rains waited, and the coming days.
Now in our tiredness we were undiversified,
human only, sunk in the primeval crouch.

Red

Small and still, the hedgehog crouched
in the shining road. He had accomplished
little of that sluggish perilous crossing.
His prickly-proofed coat had availed him nothing.
In five miles of autumn from hamlet to village
his was the finest red, soft berries of blood
springing from nostrils and little jaws.
He was still warm. He would harden soon
in that meek posture, with two paws
at his face, as if helping death
to darken his eyes. Quiet and blind
he crouched in the sun. Exultant there sang
for a while, till it darkened and dulled,
loud as October leaves, the splendid red.

Cats Dancing

Autumn evening. The builders had gone home,
rattling away down the stony track.
Their scaffolding imposed its arbitrary frames
on rectangles of darkening sky,
darker trees and hills.
                Coming tired
from the kitchen's brightness and clatter
to sharp air in the porch, I caught
a movement, a ripple of dark on dark,
and opening the door wider could then see
three black-and-gold cats, young, wild,
hungry, yet seeming to care for nothing
but their own elegant, unpredictable
subtleties of movement.
                In their grace
the evening danced, pivoting
on the lighted house in its metal frame.
Steel and stone were one with leaf,
summer's fallen walls were one
with the rising house of winter, in the
   dancing moment.
At the slam of a door, the cats were gone.
Time was sequence again, the trees
stood back darkly. Night drew on.

Arthur

No grave, no grave for Arthur.
Beyond Camelot's rootless towers
is a truth sharing the nature of rock —
hard, grey, pock-marked, lasting;
and sharing the nature of fire —
a gleam in wilderness, a sword against ice:
and sharing the nature of food —
simple and subtle, a need, a delight.
Badon is bread, bread put into our hands.

Pwll yr Afallen (Apple Tree Pool)

'Come to the apple tree pool!' she called,
running down to its green deeps.
But when she paused on the petalled shore
he was gone, hidden again
among brittle branches of laughter
on the dry hill. Slowly she stepped
alone into the water, and took its coldness
into her silence.
           In the arid lightness
of barren trees he awaited
her sure return. A small wind off the pool
put its arms round him, unrebuffed,
momentarily bringing the moist scent
of an apple-blossom shore.

Lighting Candles

Tonight, after storm, lighting candles,
I remember a picture I have seen
of Indian women at night
launching candles on leaf-boats
to float away downstream,
carrying prayers into the dark.

Tonight, lighting candles, I think
of the dark faces, the dwindling lights,
night closing back, the water
black again, reflections gone,
boats all sailed away, and the prayers
now rising from some further reach
of the sacred river. Out of sight
the dancing end of the little flames.

Tonight I light candles.
What prayers were waiting
for these new bodies of fire?
Standing outside, I see
upon a dark and turbulent sky
my house launched, with a freight of light.

Safaddan

(Many stories are told of Llyn Safaddan — Llangorse Lake — in Breconshire. The River Llynfi, which flows through it, is said never to mingle its waters with those of the lake. There are tales of a city buried under the lake. The birds of Safaddan sing only for the rightful heir to the throne of Wales. Giraldus says that three knights once put this tradition to the test. The two Anglo-Normans got no response to their commands, but for Gruffydd ap Rhys ap Tewdwr every bird cried aloud and beat its wings.)

Through bruised reeds my boat thrusts
into open water. First light broke thin mist
and was broken in a scatter of brightness
on the grey lake. In the depths
Llynfi coursed, eternally separate,
spurning the lake-waters beyond
intangible banks of its own force.
Silent lay the drowned city of legend
with its aqueous colonnades.

I had never seen the lake so thronged with birds
or known them so quiet. Hundreds there were,
out on the water, on the island,
and secret among the reeds.
On the further shore, three horsemen
rode to the lake's edge. Two dismounted,
each in turn shouting over the water—
I could not hear the words. From all
that intricate pattern of stilled wings
and watchful eyes, not one bird startled up.
The shouting sank dully into the lake.

Now the third rider, tall on a tall white horse,
slowly paced down to the hushing waters,
dismounted, knelt in prayer. I shipped my oars
and was quiet as the birds. When he stood
in the growing sunlight, knowledge came to me.
I knelt in the boat. He called.

All round me, suddenly were wings
beating the water, rustling the reeds,
and a thousand songs of homage rose.
My boat rocked in the joyful surge
of Llynfi's invisible stream, my ears
were dazed with triumphant proclamations
of sunken bells, and louder and louder
the All Hails of Safaddan's birds.
Lake and kingly rider and host of birds,
and I with them, were caught up into the sun.

Fragmented sun on sliding water:
reed-beds thick at the lake's verge:
the island low astern. Three distant riders
dwindling on a path away from the shore.
Tired, I reached for the oars.
I had never seen so many birds
on the lake. They were lifting, one by one
or dense in wedge-shaped flights.
It was quiet. There was only
my oars' creak-and-plash
and the soft rush of departing wings.

Penillion

Remembering the one fine day
in weeks of rain, I tried to tell
how we had seemed to live
a summer in a day.
'We', I wrote, 'we'.
Reading, perhaps you wonder
if you then thought or felt
anything that might justify
my tentative pronoun. It may be
less was shared than the word
seemed to proclaim. And yet
even thoughts as separate as ours
ran alongside each other happily
in the penillion of that sunny day.

Carved Capital

Hands divined the forms
trapped in the stone tree, and gave
the permitted cuts that freed them.
They oozed out, squamous, pot-bellied,
beaked, muzzled, footed, clawed,
and took up their grotesque eternal pose.

One, man-shaped, too slow escaping,
caught by the sculptor's down-tools moment,
stayed half-pillar for ever,
stretching a splayed hand roofwards,
blank hands and twisted mouth
an agonised and lasting comment.

At his locked feet a little rabbit,
eyes bulging and ears down,
joined the shape of its perpetual fear
to the grotesqueries, frustration, pain,
that high on a tree in the stone forest
bodied again the pattern of celebration.

Flying Kites

At dusk across the winter water-meadows
I see a huge star, dingy red and yellow,
wedged between fence and tree —
a kite, wind-ragged, clumsy-framed.
This is the one that never flew,
the spectacular cumbrous failure
a Dutchman made, last summer.
His girl would sit at the tent-door,
painting again and again from across the river
the house Bryndolau, not beautiful to me
till seen in her small careful watercolours —
sunlit brown, grey, green, blue
laid thick, intense as oil.
'She will hang them in our house',
he said, 'This pleases me'.
I too was pleased, for swart Bryndolau
in Amsterdam, chosen and translated.
Above, six kites flew, far, far away,
seeming to have escaped. Minute by minute
summer was wound in on an invisible cord.

The half-bare ribs of the broken kite
frame a chill river, a tentless meadow.
Faan, Marion, come again
when, colours taut on a braced frame,
another year's adventure takes the skies
on cord so fine it vanishes into blue
from summer-dazzled eyes.

Heol y Mwyn (Mine Road)

Butting the wet wind, we stumbled
along Heol y Mwyn. The sky
trawled for us with nets of drizzle
grey as the lead mined once
in the wilderness upstream.
Soaked, blinded, we crouched for refuge
in an old adit.
                    'Listen!' you said.
Now we could hear not only
the shush of rain over the shaggy surface
of the hill, but somewhere far within it
the hollow fall of water into water,
the unceasing enigmatic speech
of depth and darkness.
                    The wind veered,
the sky drew in its nets, empty.
Freely we walked up a sunny valley.
Our lightest words had now
more gentleness, since we had known,
together, the chill uneasy sound
of the hill's hidden waters, falling,
falling, for ever into dark.

A Slight Stroke

For years there had come to him,
always unpredictably,
the sense of morning on bare hills —
sun, great stones, larks rising —
a promise spelt obscurely
in the land's lines, and answered
by silent amens of the heart.

Those years ended; when,
he could not say — with youth perhaps,
or at the clouding-over of love,
or in the heavy plodding
along a digressive track,
after some unremembered
misreading of the compass.

Now his death had touched him
for the first time, brushing face,
arm, thigh, with gentle fingers,
promising return.
He felt within himself the cold
of great stones black on a bare hill
after moonlight, before dawn.

He knew this land. He rested
in its chill dusk, and waited
for the first springing up
and the remembered song
of larks, with sunlight on their wings.

Girls Laughing

I can remember laughing like that.
Two girls, folding a sheet
down there in the sun,
stagger with laughter, willingly lose
to a snatching breeze, to breathlessness,
to bulging unstable exuberance
stretched between them.
Sheet-corners escape, flap snapping.
Tugged off balance by swell and jerk
of uncontrollable life,
two girls, weeping, laugh and laugh.

School Time

Down from a farmyard on the hill
wind blows laughter, shouts,
barking, tractor's rattle.
Wind like a chivvying dog
drives muddled noise down fields
and momentarily pens it here
at the derelict school. Fleetingly,
inchoate sound takes old shapes —
alphabet, tables, prayer,
generations all together chanting.

It is cold, cold, and the little ones
can't hold their pencils. They cry
with eyesmart in wet-wood smoke.

On a good day, the Colonel calls.
'Clean pinafores and happy faces',
he approves. The children sing
heartily for him, as they would
for anyone; they like the feeling.

Walter snatches caps in the yard
and pinches Beti; she squeals and sneaks.
'Fit for reformatory school,
like the rest of his family',
says Miss James, and the cane hisses.

Tomos is chattering still.
He had to write 'Talking'
fifty times; now a year
not his gives him again
a moment's voice.

Miss Morgan is coughing.
The Infants are too cold and weepy
for listening to 'A Snowflake'.
Miss Morgan will soon leave,
'with great regret'; a film
has started to rise and fall
before her eyes, and the cough
hurts her. Summer was good.
Between shearings, pupils
attended well. She and her class
would sit by the river
for lessons on 'Sheep' and 'Hills'.
The hotly-dressed children
chewed grass and stared.

Sound shakes with shifting wind.
At the farm, the tractor stops.
Men and dogs go up the hill,
their voices passing with those others
into the fullness of silence.

Stop

(Abíshiktaparda writes that no beauty ever stops the monk,
'for he knows something more beautiful than all beauty')

What is it like to be
never stopped by beauty,
knowing something more beautiful?

By the altar, slate tablets
darkly enrich the wall,
carved script curling to celebrate
the obscure.
                    Outside,
on a sunny tombstone,
a fat green caterpillar promenades,
shiny black head like a pinching shoe
at the end of a bulging leg.

Laboriously, the earth turns.
The caterpillar goes home
into hogweed and scabious.
Sunlight moves eastward up the nave,
stroking dim names.
Richard, Harriet, Huw,
have you answers now?

My hand follows the flow
of lettering, slides over slate,
savours the rasping ruggedness
of the wall.
                    Such love
out of its very disproportion
breeds, miniscule as lichen, trust,
nurtured by this old silent place.

I go out into low sunlight,
content to be dazzled, momentarily
knowing no stop, momentarily
seeing in that bright blindness,
plain to read as a child's alphabet,
the hieroglyphs of beauty.

Gone Out

They have gone out.
The old house and the new
are silent. Indifferent sheepdogs
bark perfunctorily, back away
to muddy recesses of the yard
or slink through broken doors
into the dusk of barns.

On the hill-brow is reared
the new house, empty as yet.
Its white eyes look south
across the river. Garden, trees,
the litter of life, are still to come,
in years that spread before it
like the huge plain and skyline mountains.

The old house, not derelict yet,
stands on the yard.
On flaking steps to the tall porch
are tubs of flowers, their petals
riffled by a breeze that speaks
long and obscurely in shade-sycamores.
Windows reaching from ground
to shabby eaves accept
the farmyard with its fringe
of blue sacks, yellow tins,
its bulk of malthouse and granary,
the boast of Richard Price who built this Pile —
strong lines of wealth achieved and burgeoning.

Only the idle dogs are here
in flesh, warm, muddy-coated.
Everyone has gone out.

Journeys

I have forgotten stations we stopped at,
how old I was, how long the journey,
who sat opposite, how bags were stowed,
which wind-groomed White Horse
we galloped past, everything
but the rattling race of the train
through landscapes of anticipation,
and, now, one scene — a hillside meadow
below woods, a grey house
at the edge of the trees.

This was the destination
I at once wanted, hung out
into ear-aching wind to hanker after,
was hurried far away from,
forgot for years.
                        From what stop
on what journey comes the memory
of arrival at dusk, candle to bed,
(I a child in the loved house)?
Woken by sound that swelled
from dream to day, I ran
to the deepset window, watched
below the meadow blue with harebells
the train pass by, and waved to a child
who leaned out, longingly it seemed,
smaller and smaller, gone in a moment.
I turned then, ran downstairs, forgot.

Defences

Here and there everywhere
at all hours
are battenings-down,
nailings-up, buttressings,
reinforcings. Here,
chain-saws sound from the forest;
across the fields
far-off tapping starts again —
fence-post, stockade. Claps
of blasting from quarries
splinter miles of air. Clinking
sharp-soft as bird-call
may be distant heaping
of stone on stone.
Those old walls on the hill,
growing once more from grass,
are one row higher each dawn.
There were lights up there
again last night.
                    Hope
chooses its omens; the heron heads
for better weather,
upstream or down.
Hold your breath. Hear
the patching of the world:
the shoring-up of burrows,
the grasses digging in.

Kindred

I am still a mile or two
from the source. In spite of myself
I hear the stony flow of the stream
as speech, though not about anything
I know. No bleating, no bird-call;
the only other sound is a breeze
over molinia-grass. It is hard
not to think of a sigh.

On either hand the shallow slope
of the bank steepens, further up,
to a low hill; behind that
rises high land. Nothing seems to grow
for miles but long pale grass
in ankle-turning clumps. My mind
sees little horns of moss on the moors,
cups of lichen on grey rocks,
red-green of whinberry leaves.

Round the next curve of the stream
low broken walls delineate a life
almost beynd my imagining.
Something calls, with a voice
seeming at first as alien
as the stream's, yet inescapable,
and after a while more like
the calling of kindred,
or my own voice echoing
from a far-off encompassing wall.

Last Words

They came for his last counsel,
saying 'Tell us now, tell us,
sum your life for us before you go.
We need the right question,
the sufficient answer.'

He turned his head stiffly on the pillow,
and muttered of a curving wall
and moss on stone, of wind in the hedge
by the top gate, the stir and trample
of uneasy mares. He whispered
of a russet hill across the river,
and on the bank one golden tree.

'It is too late,' they said,
'he is babbling.' They touched his hand,
and went away.

He felt the resistance of stone,
the fragile antennae of moss
and its plushy deeps. He heard
a breeze in the hazel, and soft snorting
of gentled mares. At the river,
whirl upon whirl rose over him
the golden leaves, a visual song,
balance of phrase and phrase,
question and answer.

Banquet

(At the time of the 19th-century religious revivals it was said of two old
North Breconshire women, 'The Revival was a banquet for them.')

Their youth was poor and barren as the land.
The mould that should have formed them women
held some flaw, broke early,
spilling them out to harden into things
men's eyes would never rest on
except with scorn.
                They were strong, though.
Fighting their stony patch
on its shelf of rock, they won.
The mound-encircled garden was rough, plain,
growing food, not flowers; yet as they touched
the juicy crispness of new sap-filled leaves
they learned a kind of tenderness.

By rushlight at the dark of the year,
when knitting-pins made winter music,
they could remember those great skies
spread lordly-wise above them when they wandered
hill-pastures, scratting grey tough wool
from fence and thorn.
                Year after year
came back thaw, singing, airy softness,
pulsing of the blood, to tease and mock,
then gale and fall of leaf and snow
to tell them what they knew too well.

Then, when they were almost old, he came.
He preached in the river-meadow
to crowds who wept and begged and leapt,
cried 'Glory, glory!', fell
foaming on the rough tussocks of grass.

He seemed to speak softly, yet from the hill
they heard, and from their hut came
fearfully, like unhandled ponies.
He looked up, smiled. They were unused to love.
This thing seemed other than the rut and musk
most knew (not they). Stumbling,
each clutching the other on the sliding stones,
they took the short cut down.

That was the start of it — their banqueting-time,
wine of God, and gold, and bath
of sweetest milk, damask tent
and bed of silk, lemon-grove,
low-hung moon, summer, subtle song,
their rest, their dawn, their piercing love.

The dark time came again. They rattled logs
into flame, and shadows walked the wall.
They grew old, hunched over the hearth.
One muttered words he taught,
the other joined her in prayer,
catching at the rags of a memory. Snow
sifted under the door. Each stretched her hands
to the fire, like a beggar,
and waited for the placing in her palm
of a small dole of love.

Cat and Skull

Here is the skull of a young ram,
small slightly-curving horns
longer than they would seem
if springing from curly wool.
Perched on a tree-stump chopping-block,
its empty-socketed, broken-nosed face
is turned to stream and hills.
Tiny busy creatures scurry
into and from its cavities.

Towards it saunters the golden-eyed cat
in her pride of fur, her splendour
of marmalade, tabby and white.
Her head tilts, her paw is up to pat
at the grey-white, meatless remembrancer.
She topples it, casually, feeling no need
for confrontation. In the spread-whiskered,
plump contentment of her here and now
she pads on, not hungry, but always reserving
the right to kill. The skull
lies upside down in the grass.
Sun warms it a little, as it does
tree-stump and grass and the cat's fur.

Edward Bache Advises His Sister

(A found poem from a letter of 1802, written from Ludlow)

Dear Sister,
Although I have no reason
to suspect you of misconduct,
yet my affection and solicitude
will, I hope, excuse these lines
of brotherly advice.
Being visited by men
who profess themselves your admirers,
and not under the protection of your parents,
you are now at the most critical period
in the life of a woman.

Young, inexperienced, unsuspicious,
fond of flattery (as what woman is not),
she too often falls a victim to those worst of men
who, with the aid of oaths, protestations,
and promise of marriage,
seduce her from the paths of virtue,
rob her of her virginity,
and leave her to lament her credulity
in the most abject state of wretchedness,
deserted by her acquaintance,
reviled and scoffed at by her enemies,
a reproach to her friends,
a disgrace to her family,
and, far worse than all of these,
condemned by her own conscience!
The remainder of her life
must be miserable indeed.

If ever you find yourself in danger
of falling into this pit,
think only of the picture I have drawn
and you will shrink with horror
from the dreadful prospect,
and reflect with pleasing terror
on your happy deliverance
from the jaws of a monster so hideous.
Again, dear sister, let me advise you
not to throw yourself away.
You are yet very young,
neither ugly nor deformed,
of a creditable family,
and not entirely destitute of fortune.
Not that I would have you consider yourself
of more consequence than you are,
but I would deter you from doing
that which is beneath you.
Your very affectionate Brother,
Edward Bache.

Voyage

You would have liked, you said,
to live by the sea.
I think you had caught sight,
long ago, of the glass tower
in the midst of the sea,
and men on the tower
who did not answer your calling.
It was not really a house by the sea
you wanted, but embarkation.

Now at last you are committed
to the voyage. Rain-dark and spume
hide your dwindling ship.
In a shaft of storm-light
something gleams glassily to westward.
Let me think only
of landfall for you, and discount
the hundred stories of doom
bedevilling our ventures.

I see a hill rise out of the dark sea,
and you climbing to the tower.
I know your heart and know it set at last
towards the possiblity of welcome.

Llyn y Fan Fach

Two women pick their way down from the lake,
sandals filling with sharp stones
or slithering on the hot grass verge.
'Not far now,' they call. I can see
the black-red cliffs of the farther shore
rearing above knolls ahead. On the left,
far up to the craggy skyline,
parched pasture is stretched like yellow skin
on a fevered body. The sky
is a strident blue; there is no shade here,
no glint of healing water yet.

She has gone back long ago into the lake,
the lady of legend, taking
her mild cows and small snorting calves
and her own dark softness.
A gentleness three times struck with iron
is gone. The harsh track leads at last
to sombre cliffs, shadowed water.
On the shore I feel the breath of a breeze
from who knows what chill corridor.
Later, down the track, I call
to those who climb 'Not far'.

Church in the Rain

Wrapped in rain the small church
stands high. There are no graves
on the north, the devil's side,
where blown soaking trees
transmit his cajoling cry
Let me in in in
To the south the sober congregation
of stones endures in grey uprightness.
The land slopes down into mist.

Inside the church I switch on lights,
shut the door on that crying in the trees.
Now there is the sweetness
of being dry when it rains,
having light after drearness.
A soft confusion of voices
laps up against this refuge.
Hide me, they say, comfort me
I want that which is no dream
That which I want is no dream
I want   I want

Thomas Powell died;
Catherine his mournful wife
cries and wants. Wine stands
in a vessel near the altar.
All ye who travail come
They are coming in from the rain
crying Save me, love me
and always that other wails
Let me in

As I leave, rain slacks. From the porch
I see the world in negative,
land eerily pale, sky black. Tonight
in my lighted room I feel the power
of that beleaguered place, miles away,
lightless in a night of rain and voices.
I want that which is no dream
That which I want is no dream
I want   I want
Let me in

Heavily falls, on and on, the rain

Fossils

We are finding fossils
in pebbles by the lake — minute skeletons,
inconceivably old. What such creatures
made of life is also inconceivable.
Robin is six, and prefers the plop
of pebbles into water, now,
and the skittering bounce of flat ones
over the surface, now.

Best are the small frogs, coral and green,
that half-hide in and out of weed
or sit in the shallows, placidly pulsing,
seeming to gaze intelligently up
at our refracted faces.
They are beautifully dressed in cold flesh,
aeons away from bony patterns
in layered rock; and better, I feel —
obstinately, like the child — better.

Friends' Room

They would make no claim for their quiet room.
Yet if there came a guilt long implanted,
ignorant of itself, bent on blackness,
here if anywhere it might be healed,
here where beyond the window
an apple-tree presses in —
soft-blossoming white forgiveness,
huge and branching, not content to stay
on the other side of the glass.

The Ferret

Intent, they hardly noticed me,
the one child there.
I don't remember the ferret-man,
only the sly movement of hand to pocket,
the swift slinking beast thrust
into the hut, cleared of its hens.

Sounds, sights I recall
go quickly by in fragments,
like a not-too-explicit film
condensing violence — squeals,
blood on white, blood on grey,
bitten corpses glimpsed,
overlapping in a bucket:
the little killer retrieved,
tucked away, still splashed with red.

What I remember clearly
and with a living repulsion
is the woman, grey-haired, red-eyed,
in a long white apron, who screamed and wept,
laughed and screamed, throwing her apron
up over her head, but not going,
staying there, looking again, screaming again.

It was the rhythmic sweep of the apron
that frightened me, the disappearance
of her long face with its wet red eyes —
that, and the hideous sound of her horror.

Later, I tried to tell, and was not heard.
'She cried,' was all I kept saying.
They laughed, puzzled, soothing me
about the shrill necessary
bloody deaths that had not appalled me,
promising me the ferret had gone away.

Hawthorn at Digiff

When I was a child, hawthorn
was never brought into our house.
It was godless to throw a pinch
of spilled salt, or dodge ladders,
yet no-one ever carried in
the doomy sweetness of red may or white.

Down there by the river,
shivering with heat, is Digiff,
a house full of hawthorn. The tree
grows in the midst of it, glowing
with pale pink blossom, thrusting
through gaps that were windows,
reaching up where no roof
intervenes between hearth and sky.

On the hill, sun has hardened
old soggy fields below the bluebell woods.
Rusty wire sags from rotten posts.
Outcrops, couchant dinosaurs, share
rough comfort with a few unshorn sheep.
Below, gardens have left their mark.

I bring a thought into this day's light
of Esther and Gwen, paupers:
Rhys and Thomas, shepherds: John Jones,
miner of copper and lead:
who lived here and are not remembered,
whose valley is re-translated
by holiday bathers across the river,
lying sun-punched: by me:
by men who keep a scatter of sheep
on the old by-takes.

At Digiff is hawthorn on hearth and bed-place.
Seen close, the tree is flushed
with decay. Sick lichened branches
put out in desperate profusion
blossom that hardly knows
an hour of whiteness before slow dying
darkens it. This is that glowing tree
of doom and celebration,
whose cankered flowers I touch
gently, and go down to the ford.

Lichen, Cladonia Fimbriata

This little scaly thing,
fibrous lichen, taker of peat-acid
and the rotten juice of dead trees,
grows lowly, slowly, on bog-earth
or the scant soil of crevices,
and holds up to the air its fruit
in tiny fantastic goblets.

Might not this pallid creeping thing,
that needs for food only the sour,
sparse and corrupt, be late to go? —
too small and too tenacious
to be torn off by the dusty wind,
and offering in final celebration
its little tainted chalices?

Train to the Sea

When she was old, contented,
I think, with her inland home,
she said 'One of these mornings
I'm going to get on a train
by myself, and go to the sea.'
It became just something she would say,
repeated with no urgency,
little conviction. No-one felt any need
to help her set out on that small adventure.
No-one thought she would do it, or even
that she truly wanted to go.

Yet after she died, I found her list
of trains to the sea, crumpled a bit
and thumbed, as if she had often
peered at it, making her plans.
But always in the end it seemed
a formidable, rash and lonely thing,
that little journey, and she calmed
her heart with small domestic things,
or saw rain coming, or heavy heat, and stayed.

Turning Inland

Hard to leave you on the cold sands,
your back to slow-shifting dunes,
waiting, your gaze on the sea's patterns.

Hard to think you not alone;
if there are others on that beach
they are not such as I can see.

Hard to know it good that I
should turn inland, keeping the gift
of your paradoxical presence.

Pausing

What do they make of it? Down they come
from the hill, damp maps flapping, anoraks
brightly outfacing the weather, walking-boots
dark with bog-water. Suddenly
the sun comes out; hoods are pushed back,
laces loosened. Here it is, the valley
they headed for, spying on the map
slackening contours, green-edged meanders,
and the thin line of road beyond
plunging on into brown, more brown.
Here it is; their most wishful imaginings
prove true. Happily they pause
by the stream. Soon to be gone, they need
put nothing to the test. Stepping out,
they will be able to say,
luxuriating, 'If we could only stay!'

Slate-quarry, Penceulan

I had known the quarry for years —
dark hills of broken slate: round hole,
high up, of an adit: a black
unfenced shaft down by the river:
and, reassuringly, above it all
a strip of untroubled green catching the sun.

When I spoke of the place to a man
who well knew it, that bland field
was the danger he warned of —
not slipping slate, not the tunnel's whisper
of shift and sag. The high field,
said he, spoke no word of its peril.
He had seen horses, dogs, men
skeltering along it, and no harm done.

But he had been inside the hill. He drew
no chart; from his words I read
the unfading map spread in his mind.
I know the three-branched tunnel now,
the water-barrier, the fall-blocked road,
the third way with its rusty rails
reddish in torchlight, opening out
into a chamber whose functional hugeness
amazes, whose dark hollowness
rears up close under sunny grass.

My mind makes a tree, rising out of the dark
of that hidden hall, breaking the shell
of the hill, flowering high in the air,
binding blackness to light. Its petals cling
in the manes of horses that innocently go
galloping on the green brittle hill.

Solstice

December moon swells:
Virgo rises in the east.
Behind early curtains we hide
from gentle exacting light
in controllable brightness,
and tame to tinsel patterns
the immortality-tree.
We are as adamantly shut,
as helpless, as the solstice-door,
that will not escape
the imminent shattering of locks
at the push of a child's hand.

Acknowledgements

to the following publications, in which a
number of these poems first appeared:

Anglo-Welsh Review
Aquarius
Bananas
Candelabrum
Country Life
Country Quest
Countryman
New Welsh Review
Planet
Poetry Book Supplement
Poetry Wales
Window on Wales